Vampire Sapien

Rebuild The Race

I0157049

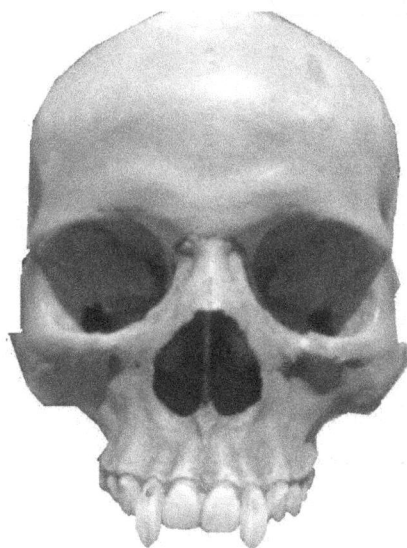

Vampire Sapien

Rebuild The Race

By

D T Pollard

Essence Bestselling Author

Other works

By

D T Pollard

Rooftop Diva – A Novel of Triumph After Katrina (fiction)

Fools' Heaven – Love, Lust and Death Beyond the Pulpit (fiction)

TARP TOWN U S A – The Recession That Saved America

OBAMA GUILTY OF BEING PRESIDENT WHILE BLACK

The Mark Unmasked

Publish Free For Kindle Today Sell Worldwide Tomorrow

Vampire Sapien   D T Pollard

Book Express books may be ordered
through
booksellers or by contacting
Book Express
P.O. Box 541651
Grand Prairie, TX 75052
www.DTPollard.com
dtpollard@dtpollard.com
This is a work of non-fiction

United States of America

Vampire Sapien   D T Pollard

Genealogical Tree of Humanity.

The Evolution of Man

Vampire Sapien   D T Pollard

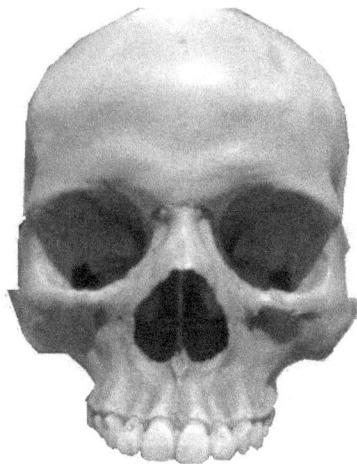

Human – Homo Sapien

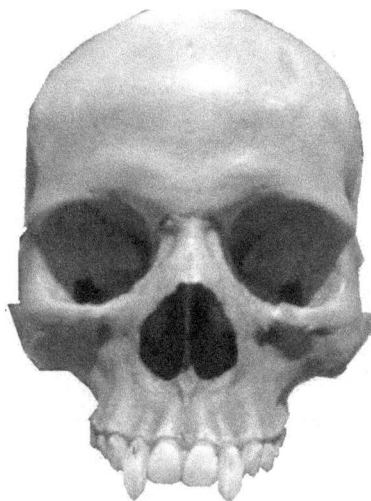

Vampire – Vampire Sapien

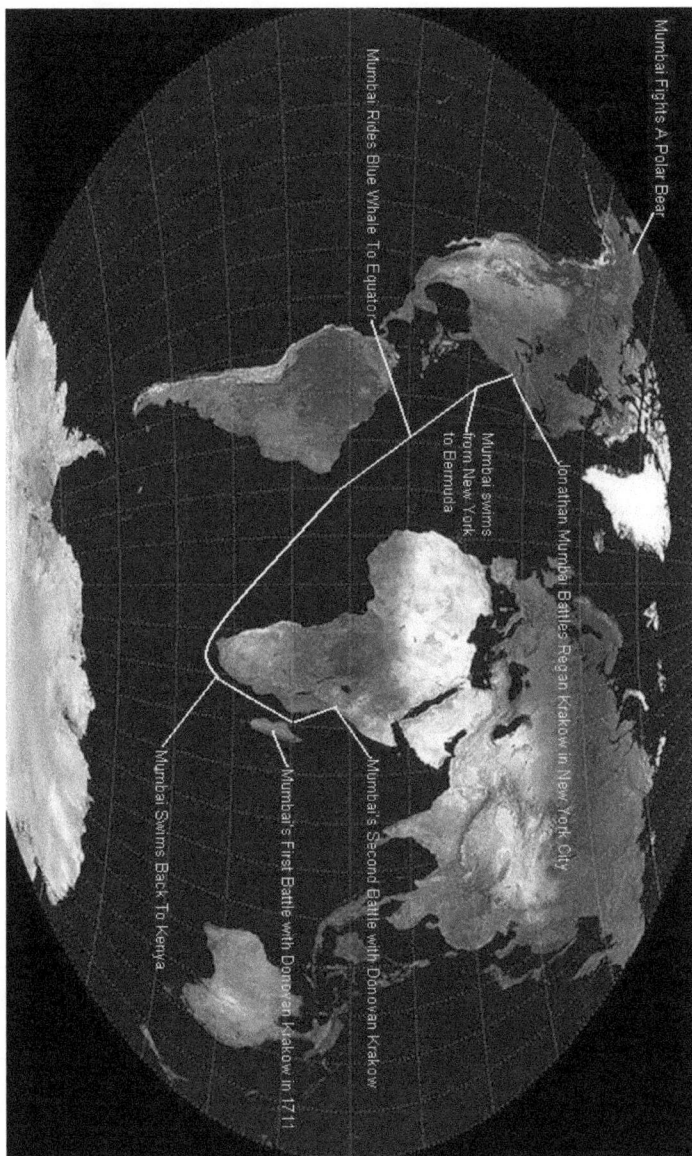

Vampire Sapien   D T Pollard

It is my time
I am a Vampire Sapien
I hunger
I thirst
I am not romantic nor noble
I am like the lion
I stalk like a leopard
I smell humans in the air
I detect one lagging behind
I have an opening
I strike with ruthless efficiency
I clamp my fangs down over her windpipe
I feel her body going limp
I see eyes glowing in the distance
I know it is Mukanda, the male lion
I hear his rumble
I recognize his yielding of the kill
I will hunt with him another day
I will leave the carcass to his discretion
I feed
I am a Vampire Sapien

D T Pollard

Vampire Sapien   D T Pollard

Act 1

It was a surreal sight
Two combatants faced each other under
shimmering moonlight
Lost in the vastness of Africa's boundless
grasslands
The king of beasts stared down a solitary
man
Yet this human expressed no fear
He crouched and faced the lion Mukanda
with his face expressing a sneer
With his body naked as when he was born
This man was of no known norm
Mukanda, the lion, was in his prime
Pure muscle and claws reacted when it was
time
This man met the beast's powerful leap
Both combatants clashed and tumbled down
into a convulsing heap
The fury and power was sufficient to
astound
Yet in this remoteness, surely, no witnesses
were around
Razor-like claws ripped at this human's
flesh
Yet this man stood and slammed his fists
into the lion's chest
The sound was visceral enough to cause
blood to run cold

Yet a man wrestled this lion to the earth
with an inhuman hold
What manner of mortal could withstand the
might
Of the male lion Mukanda on a moonlit
African night
Although they reasoned to be alone
Secluded eyes watched and recorded the
raging battle going on
The two combatants separated without a hint
of hate
Deciding this epic battle was at a stalemate
The pair turned and ran until they could be
seen no longer
Together, hunting for prey to satiate their
boundless hunger
Later the world would look on with amazed
eyes
One hundred million viewers gasped in
wonder at why this man survives
Who, or what was he, where had this person
been
Did he spring from the same ancient garden
in Eden
Scholars gathered from around the globe
Determined to unravel a mystery and sever
its hold
This could not be something true that a
camera caught
No man could survive a male lion's
onslaught

Vampire Sapien

D T Pollard

Yet there was not a hint of deceit
This manlike beast was a nightmare humans
see in their sleep
This left authorities with no choice
To Africa they must go to quell the public's
voice

Vampire Sapien   D T Pollard

His name was Jonathan Mumbai
He was alive when Shaka Zulu died
Jonathan saw an eastern star's shining light
He watched three wise men traveling with
his own sight
On every continent he had walked
Every manner of prey, man and beast, he
had stalked
Then to escape human fears
Mumbai went to sleep for three hundred
years
Now was the time for him to come alive and
feel
Mukanda, the lion, would hone his skills
Jonathan Mumbai was not some nonexistent
mythical form
He was a Vampire Sapien from the day he
was born
Mumbai possessed dominant genes
He was the last of his kind ever seen
Two thoughts possessed his mind
He needed to feed and breed with
humankind
For his virus there was no cure
His offspring would be ninety-nine percent
pure
In order to regain his glorious power
The Vampire would feed every hour
Vampire Sapiens do not cower from sunlight
Garlic and crosses do not cause them to take
flight

Vampire Sapien

D T Pollard

They do not fly, disappear or assume animal
form
Yet they are far from a true human born
Air is the one element they need to survive
Without oxygen, they can not remain alive
Yet the air does not always need to be
breathed in
It can be absorbed through pores in their
skin
How does one destroy something so far
apart?
He does not die from a stake through the
heart
The head must be severed and consumed by
fire
The brain is the organ that controls his living
desire
He must be destroyed and his life force from
him torn
The virus spread at his will is airborne
Jonathan Mumbai looked like any other man
Standing over six-feet tall with skin of dark
tan
He was long, lean and with sinewy muscles
his body flowed
Mumbai appeared human and no one would
know
Unless another felt his bite or crushing blow

Mankind's saviors arrived on the African
plains
They established camp and planned their
game
A scientist, naturalist, cameraman and guide
A mobile laboratory and small arsenal were
at their side
Ronald Mason was a scientist extraordinaire
He was sure of a hoax and would clear the
air
Joan Francis was a naturalist with blond
locks and blue eyes
She lived her life exploring and sleeping
under clear skies
Miles Smith was the man that filmed a lion
fighting a man
Miles Smith held that magic camera in his
hands
Abasi Karanja was a tracker of high
reputation
No man or beast could escape him in this
nation
This band set out into the wild
Their expectations were not high but
surprisingly mild

Jonathan Mumbai walked with a long stride
Mukanda the lion was at his side
Mumbai held wonders that never ceased
He could understand both man and beast
"What are you, who calls himself Mumbai
Other naked apes would surely die
My claws ripped you open and went deep
within
Yet you stood tall and smashed your fists
into my skin"
"I am Jonathan Mumbai
I am a Vampire Sapien
I hunger
I thirst
I am not romantic nor noble
I am like the lion
I stalk like a leopard
I have been alive for centuries
I came from the same garden called Eden
My ancestors were stricken from the great
religious books
Yet they thrived and survived
I am the last of my kind
My destiny is to resurrect my race
Vampire Sapiens must assume their rightful
place"
"Mumbai, tomorrow I must leave you
It is time for me to do what a male lion must
do
My strength is at a high tide
I must go and secure my own pride

Vampire Sapien   D T Pollard

An old king lives nearby
Before the next sunset, he must die
We will hunt Cape buffalo tonight
I need strength for my looming fight"

The exploration group set up their remote outpost
It was near where lions gathered the most
Deep into the dark of night
Abasi Karanja saw a startling sight
"Wake up," Abasi said to the rest of the crew
"I'll start the camera," Miles Smith said that was what he would do
"My God," Joan Francis uttered at what she saw
How long would it be before her blood would thaw
Ronald Mason could not conjure words to speak
His hairs stood on end and curiosity was at its highest peak
Because unfolding before them on the plains below
Was a display of what had to be nature's greatest show
Mukanda the lion prowled around a ring of solid horns
A circle of Cape buffalo had formed
Then a figure whose life spanned over two thousand years
Walked alongside Mukanda with no fears

A massive bull rushed forward at full speed
from the pack
Mumbai the vampire braced for the collision
and tensed his back
The ground thundered as the charging one-
ton beast galloped forward at full speed
Nothing but massive muscles and boned
horns directed where this impact would lead
The bull was full of rage and dipped his
massive head
A normal man would surely be dead
Jonathan Mumbai grasped the beast by the
curve of his horns
The vampire slid backwards into a bed of
thorns
Never did he release his grip
The massive buffalo gored, slashed and
ripped
The enrage beast pounded Mumbai into the
earth
The Vampire Sapien marshaled his strength
for all he was worth
Then with a bloodcurdling sound
Mumbai, the vampire threw the great beast
to the ground
As the animal rolled onto his back
The mighty male lion joined in the attack
Mukanda came out of the darkness with a
bounding leap
This beast would never again rise to his feet

Vampire Sapien   D T Pollard

The fangs of the lion clamped around the
bull's windpipe
Soon his life ebbed away and he would no
longer fight
Then as if to end the game
Mumbai opened his mouth, bit down and out
the windpipe came
The observing group was shaken to their
cores
Some of their stomach contents were
expelled to the earthen floor
Even in the midst of his gorging feed
A scent came to the vampire that he must
heed
The scent of human flesh was sweet on the
winds of the wild
He could also detect a woman with child
This was something that clouded his mind
The blood of a not-yet-born would extent his
time

Suddenly Mumbai did rise and stare
He gazed towards the succulent scent in the
air
His eyes could not detect what his nostrils
found
He turned back to the beast on the ground
"He looked and knows that we are here,"
Miles Smith said with a hint of fear
"I zoomed in and captured his face
I think it is time we left this place."
Miles said as if to warn of danger
"Nonsense" Ronald Mason said to this
stranger
"Worry not, I have an elephant gun.
Why should we turn tail and run?"
Abasi, the guide, said with pride
"This man beast is the one that should hide
We will capture him and the world will
behold
This hideous freak and shower us with gold
My name will be legend from deserts hot to
mountains cold
The greatest-hunter-ever-known's story will
be forever told"
Abasi was becoming intoxicated with power
He failed to understand the danger of that
dark hour

Vampire Sapien   D T Pollard

Mumbai lay beside Mukanda as they were
engorged from their feast
The meal was plentiful from the vanquished
beast
"Mukanda tomorrow I must leave
You have your own destiny to achieve
Let me tell you how I came to be the last
Vampire Sapiens were meant to be the
ruling class
There was one who betrayed our race
He sought world conquest and we almost
vanished without a trace
His name was Donovan Krakow
Vampire Sapien born, he was, just as I am
now
I told Krakow we just needed to preserve
our kind
He laughed and said that I was weak of
mind
Donovan screamed we were born to be
kings
Humans were wretched prey and no more
than things
He raised an army composed of the pure
Ruthlessly converting humans, until their
bodies found a cure
Like the rising of the sun and moon
Many of my kind perished all too soon
I knew that Krakow had to die
Only one could defeat him and I had to try

Vampire Sapien   D T Pollard

I loathe engaging in battle with one of my
own
Our code forbids it, but all other hope was
gone
Krakow was my elder by four hundred years
To kill an original strain brought me to tears
I knew this would be the greatest of all
fights
Krakow knew ancient death techniques from
before I had sight
His bones were as dense as stone pillars
Still, I knew I had to destroy this killer
We met where no other eyes could spy
In the midst of a canyon under a summer
sky
There was no need to hide or pretend
We unleashed our true power from within
Both standing near seven feet tall
Our fangs were sharpened with intentions to
maul
I told him he had one chance to change his
ways
He spit in my face and we began to battle for
three days
We would rend each other with claws and
fangs
Our flesh would rip and often hang
One the third day my strength was
beginning to spend
I knew if I lost, my race would be at an end
It was at that point I had to decide

Vampire Sapien   D T Pollard

To allow Krakow to think I had died
I commanded my body to remove all blood
From my heart and to my limbs it did flood
I marshaled my strength and unleashed a
blow
It missed its mark and my chest was exposed
from below
Krakow would not allow that opening to go
by
He thrust his hand into my heart and I
uttered a cry
I collapsed and fell back onto the ground
Krakow leaned over me to make sure that I
would remain down
I could see his face from the corner of my
eyes
I lurched forward to his shock and surprise
It was too late and no way could he protect
My fangs from ripping and sinking into his
neck
I tasted his blood as I tightened my bite
Then I twisted my neck muscles with all of
my might
His windpipe was severed in one motion
I removed his head and later tossed it into
the ocean
Krakow was dead
A Great White Shark devoured his head
I knew what I needed to do
The human immunity needed to run its
course through

Vampire Sapien   D T Pollard

In order to allow human bodies to lose their
fears
I found a moist cave and slept for three
hundred years
Now it is my time to come back around
No memory of my virus can be found
I will be the rebirth of an ancient disease
My illness will burn, infect and do as it
pleases
My race will rise again
This time comprised of transformed men
It will take those who are weak
Cancer, aids and other diseases will peak
Man will think my virus is a cure
They will spread it and their offspring will
be pure
The weak will become strong
The future of the Vampire Sapiens will be
long"

Vampire Sapien   D T Pollard

"Vampire, a lion does not live for three
hundred years
Tomorrow I fight and have no fears
The old king will die if he stands to fight
If he flees, let him live, I might
My flame will burn hot and brief
One day, death will take me like a thief
I must ensure my genes survive
Once I am king, I will not leave his young
offspring alive
That is the way of the king of beasts
Any other life would see us cease
I can remain supreme for a few seasons
I could die for any number of reasons
An injury during the heat of a chase
A kick, bite or cut could seal my case
Go forth Mumbai, one like you I have never
seen
A Vampire Sapien seems to be caught in
between
Are you beast or man
Will your race survive, I know you believe it
can
You will need to be wary of your power
It could slowly render you insane hour by
hour"
"Lion, after we dispatched this buffalo
I detected a scent so sweet coming from
below
It was an aroma that almost brought me to
tears

Vampire Sapien　　　　　　D T Pollard

Something I have not smelled in three
hundred years
There were humans close enough to be in
the wind
My mind was distracted and now I can not
rest within
At least one of them was with child
That delicacy is enough to drive my heart
wild
There is something in the preborn blood
It extends my life and my body with energy
will flood
I feel they are near
After you take your pride, they should fear
It has been three centuries since I have been
around
There are new wonders I am sure man has
found
I will study them from afar
To understand how advanced they are
Then after I have learned what I need to
know
The woman I will take with a swift and
deadly blow
That is what I need to be truly alive
Her embryonic pup will cause me to thrive
This will be my final night

Mukanda, I know that you will prevail in
your fight
Tomorrow when you are the king anew

Vampire Sapien   D T Pollard

Remember the Vampire Sapien that dared to
hunt with you"

Vampire Sapien   D T Pollard

As the hunting pair lay down to rest
A rumbling sound thundered across the
plains and rattled their chests
The old lion king was sounding his
territorial roar
Unaware that before the next sunset, he
would breathe no more
The next day as the searing sun beat down
Mukanda walked with the vampire to secure
his crown
Suddenly the lion stopped in his tracks
The old king loomed before him and did not
turn back
Mukanda moved forward as the vampire
stood still
In this moment the old king would die or
Mukanda would be killed
Then as if some signal sounded from out of
the past
The two supreme cats charged and clashed
Never was a battle as fierce and loud
The old monarch was still strong and proud
Then from the side there was a furious rush
Another male lion joined in the crush
In confusion, Mukanda pondered who was
this other
Unknown to him the old king had a twin
brother
Mukanda was stronger than each of his
opponents alone

Vampire Sapien   D T Pollard

But together they would make him another
lion, dead and gone
Mumbai thought he would not interfere
Yet he could not see his friend die so near
The vampire ran to join the fight
He struck the second lion with all of his
might
The lion turned and roared at Mumbai with a
menacing stare
He turned to look and his brother was no
longer there
Mukanda held him down with a death bite
under his neck
The brother retreated because there was
nothing left to protect
Mukanda released his crushing hold
The battle was won and the defeated lion's
body began to go cold
"Vampire, I owe you my survival."
"It was what I had to do lion. No one should
have to face two rivals.
I leave you now and go to meet my destiny
If I see you again, I will have other Vampire
Sapiens with me."
The Vampire walked away towards the
sweet scent of mankind
The lion went to his new pride as the best
king they could find

Vampire Sapien   D T Pollard

Mumbai waited until darkness overpowered
the light
He searched for the humans with his
uncanny sight
With eyes unlike any ordinary man
He peered through the blackness just as a
night dweller can
Faint light would be gathered up
Pitch black appeared to him like dusk
Add in the reflective light of the moon
Midnight was as bright as midday noon
"There they are cowering within a stand of
trees.
Did they really think they could hide from
me?
I will feign no knowledge of their existence
They will track me with persistence
Once I have gained the information I desire
They will die under the scorching sun's fire
At least one among them is a prize
She is with child and that lights up my eyes
I will sleep tonight within their full gaze
Tomorrow I lead them to death within a
jungle maze."

"There he is sleeping under that tree
We would take him now if it were up to me
Why should we wait until some other time
The element of surprise is not on his mind,"
Abasi the tracker said with frustration he
could not hide
"Remember the male lion that was by his
side
What would we do if we tried to take him
down
That lion could leap from the shadows and
maul us to the ground
I say we capture him in the full light of day
Shoot him with a tranquilizer and haul him
away."
That was Joan Francis's suggestion
She felt it was best for their personal
protection
Three would sleep while one kept a watchful
eye
Slowly the African night passed by
Then under the rising sun
Mumbai suddenly awoke and began to run
The group scrambled from their sleep
They quickly followed the vampire in their
jeep
As they traversed the vast terrain
Their bearings, they failed to maintain
How could any man move at such speed?

Vampire Sapien   D T Pollard

This vampire ran faster than a galloping
steed
Onward the group continued to push
Then they realized they were driving
through thick bush
"There he is entering that cluster of trees
Hurry now before he flees,"
Abasi extolled and they continued forth
The trek had taken them far to the north
Suddenly their vehicle stopped with a jolt
One of the tires struck a rock and sheared a
crucial bolt
In the wasteland there was no way to
achieve a repair
Now this group was isolated and stranded
there

Vampire Sapien   D T Pollard

Mumbai knew this was the opening he
would need
Caution no longer would he heed
Stepping out into the full light of day
He stood about one hundred meters away
Abasi decided to take no chances
He raised his potent elephant gun to startled
glances
The scope had Mumbai squarely within its
sights
Abasi's finger squeezed the trigger and the
gunpowder did alight
The bullet left the chamber with inhuman
speed
It was all of the time Mumbai would need
He saw the steel plated round speeding
towards his head
Abasi was sure his target was certainly dead
The Vampire moved quickly to the right
The bullet crashed into a tree and caused the
humans much fright
Four people looked on with frightened stares
What manner of creature was this standing
there
Then a sad reality began to dawn
That the next deaths may be their own
Jonathan ran and with two leaps
He landed on their vehicle's hood with his
feet
Still as naked as the day he was born

Vampire Sapien   D T Pollard

The breath from the humans was torn
"I am Jonathan Mumbai, Vampire Sapien
pure
We are distant cousins, but I am a disease
without a cure
You can decide to live or die as you please
If you oppose me I will bring you to your
knees
I have no desire to rule your kind
My race must return and that is what I have
in mind
The woman I must take for myself
She holds the secret to my continued health
You have on day to decide
Give her to me or run and hide
I will wait one day beyond that hill
If she is not waiting for me, I will hunt you
all down for the kill."
Mumbai turned and began to run
Over a hill towards the setting sun

"What kind of nightmare have we found
ourselves in
He called himself a Vampire Sapien
This monster seemed to be almost seven feet
tall
I think he could easily kill us all
If we start walking for a full day
Possibly we could get away."
Abasi remarked in haste
Then he looked Joan in the face.
"Why do you want me to do?
I don't know anything about him, just like
you."
"What secret are you trying to hide with
stealth?
How are you the key to his future health?
Mumbai said if we gave you to him, he
would let us be
It almost sounds like a fair trade to me
After all, why should we all perish
For one woman that none of us cherish
You had better let us know as soon as you
can
Any secrets that could be driving that
grotesque man."
The scientist said with resolve
Joan was confused as to how this puzzle
could be solved
"There may be one fact that none of you are
aware

I am with child, but why would he care?"
"Don't worry we will not leave you as a
monster's sacrifice
Our best chance to survive is to move, we
can not think twice."
"Abasi, can you place a call on your radio
and ask for rescue?"
Miles asked, while knowing what they must
do
"No we are too far out for my signal to reach
a cell tower
We need to travel while there are still some
daylight hours
Each of you, take a loaded hand gun
Use them if he comes while we run
We will walk back in that direction and if
nothing has changed
After eight hours we should be within
telephone signal range
Gather up some water and food
Let us leave now so we can get as far as we
should
If this thing keeps his vow
We may have a chance to escape him now
On this journey I wish everyone well
If we don't make it, we will meet in either
heaven or hell"
Abasi, the tracker, ended his talk
By turning, moving away and they all began
to walk

Honesty was one of Mumbai's true traits
One full day he did wait
He went to where the humans were last
found
Only the vehicle was there, no one else was
around
"So they decided to run away
Those humans will rue this day
I can see the direction they did depart
I still smell their scent and hear the beating
of their hearts
If they survived the night in the wild
I will catch them and have the woman with
child
Maybe Mukanda fed them to his new pride
If so, that is the way of nature and from it no
one can hide
I will run after them and within a few hours
I will swoop down upon those hapless
beings with all of my power
I may spare one or two
I may need assistance to accomplish what I
must do
Two of them could be my first
transformations
Money and access is required to move to
another nation
I need to be where human kind lives in
abundance

Vampire Sapien   D T Pollard

I heard them speak of New York and
London
While they decided their actions racked with
fear
Their voices carried and I could hear
Yes some of them may be more valuable
than they know
They could assist me in getting where I need
to go."
Mumbai slowed in his furious pace
He saw four members ahead from the
human race
They were walking in a strung out line
One of them was lagging and falling behind
He followed for awhile, staying out of sight
Mumbai's strike would take place at night

Vampire Sapien   D T Pollard

Mumbai decided the moment had arrived
After three centuries he would be truly alive
The timid would revolt at what some see as
gory
This Vampire Sapien would be in his glory
"It is my time
I am a Vampire Sapien
I hunger
I thirst
I am not romantic nor noble
I am like the lion
I stalk like a leopard
I smell humans in the air
I detect one lagging behind
I have an opening
I strike with ruthless efficiency
I clamp my fangs down over her windpipe
I feel her body going limp
I see eyes glowing in the distance
I know it is Mukanda, the male lion
I hear his rumble
I recognize his yielding of the kill
I will hunt with him another day
I feed
I am a Vampire Sapien
I rend her abdomen to find my treasure
I find a pup, just weeks old and it is my
greatest pleasure
I don't understand what it contains inside
I feel the rush of energy as a rising tide

Vampire Sapien   D T Pollard

I have extended my life for one hundred
years
I now can progress to gaining my goals and
feeding man's fears
I see Mukanda waiting in the darkness
I rise and leave to his discretion the fate of
her carcass
I see no beauty in the human female
I am like the lion who does not admire the
beauty of a dying gazelle
I may be linked to man by distant genes
I see them as prey and converts, but nothing
in between
I will change them with my infection and
they will then know
I have elevated them from a species below."

Vampire Sapien   D T Pollard

The Vampire Sapien found the remaining
three humans on the run
One managed to shoot him with a gun
He struck the man and severed his head
The others watched as Abasi fell dead
"Humans, do not dare move
Do not waste your lives, you have nothing to
prove
It is time for me to leave this land
You will help execute my plan
I need your knowledge of this new age
After hundreds of years the world has turned
a new page
Come close so that you are near
I will not harm you, do not fear."
The two men walked as if in a trance
Mumbai stared into their eyes and lowered
his stance
A gland under his tongue pulsed and
produced a secretion
With one exhale he contaminated the air and
the men breathed in
Initially the sweet aroma was a surprise
Then a stinging sensation irritated their eyes
"You are newlings and do not yet
understand
I will teach you with my own hand
Now you must serve me
London or New York is where I need to be
I listened as you spoke of these places

Vampire Sapien   D T Pollard

With joy in your voices and smiles on your
faces
You will get me there and with great
surprise
My virus will spread and the Vampire
Sapiens will once again rise."

Vampire Sapien   D T Pollard

Act 2

It was the year of our lord of seventeen
hundred and eleven
A manlike creature was walking across the
boundless plains of his ancestral heaven
This was the original origin of mankind
A land now known as Kenya clouded his
mind
His wounds required time to heal
The last of his kind was a heavy burden to
feel
A fierce battle had raged on the island now
known as Madagascar
He killed the other of his species and had
made it this far
To look in his eyes and study his face
One would think him of the human race
Yet this one, was a close relation
Of Homo sapiens, but from a different
nation
You see there were branches of the family
tree
Humans, other primates and Vampire
Sapiens all came to be
Humans multiplied greatly and were spread
far and wide
Unknown to man Vampire Sapiens walked
by his side
This last one confronted another that was
thought to be mad

Vampire Sapien   D T Pollard

To kill a brother made him incredibly sad
Jonathan Mumbai had to decide how to
proceed
Now he was alone due to a lust for power
and greed
Donovan Krakow was the other
They never knew of a shared mother
The life of a Vampire Sapien is rich and
long
When Mumbai was born Krakow had been
for four-hundred years gone
Mumbai met Krakow and his dreams of
domination
Donovan wanted to rule humans with a vast
Vampire nation
Krakow had travel and circled the globe
Spreading the virus, but it would no longer
take hold
Humans had adapted and would no longer
convert
Those that had before began to ache and hurt
Then by the thousands they began to die
Men were frightened because no one knew
why
Man had no knowledge of their true state
He just concluded that a new plague left
death in its wake
Now it had come down to last two of the
pure
They were alone as the human body had
created a cure

Vampire Sapien   D T Pollard

Vampire Sapiens could convert man through
a virus spread on the wind
It would lie dormant and wait for a
weakness when the body could not defend
Then the changes would begin and the
conversion was sure
A human became a Vampire Sapien ninety-
nine percent pure
Mumbai learned of the deaths masses of
men
He examined the bodies and found they
were Vampire Sapiens within
After traveling the world for three complete
years
He finally found Donovan Krakow and
confirmed his fears
He tracked down Krakow in a world that
was new
Mumbai had decided what he must do
Donovan told him of his desire for the
conquest of man
Mumbai knew Krakow had to die by his
hands
Krakow had no intention to end his mission
To convert men to vampires even with the
death rate attrition
Mumbai knew he had no choice
Except to kill Krakow and silence his voice
If Krakow continued on his mad quest
Vampire Sapiens were at an end and would
disappear with the rest

Vampire Sapien   D T Pollard

The only answer was to remove the virus
from the human population
If there was ever any chance for a revived
Vampire Sapien nation
"Krakow you must stop this madness
You continued mission will only lead to
sadness."
"Mumbai you are much younger than me
You are only eighteen hundred and I am two
thousand two hundred and three
I will find humans who have never had the
virus and make them a part of us
This I swear and you can trust."
"Krakow, I can not allow you to proceed
Meet me in three months from today and I
will make you bleed
 The big island near Africa is where we will
engage in a Vampire Sapien war
The clash will be legend both near and far."
"It is done Mumbai. I will leave this new
world now
Prepare for battle for I will kill you, I vow."
Mumbai had found what he was searching
for after three days
A deep cave, that was remote, secure and
hidden from any casual gaze
The Vampire Sapien entered the
mountainside cavity
He punched at the entrance until rocks
sealed him in when felled by gravity
Mumbai buried himself and had no fears

Vampire Sapien   D T Pollard

He would not awake for three hundred years

Act 3

Mumbai learned the ways of modern man
He walked, talked and dressed to blend in as
best he can
With a false identify and documents to
match
An ancient creature learned to fly as the
attendant closed the latch
With his minions in tow
A Vampire Sapien looked down at the world
that seemed so small below
What had man conjured while he slept in an
underground cave
Doubt entered his mind about how his race
could be saved
Could he contend with modern humans and
their wonders anew?
Who knows what their killing machines
could do
This flying vessel contained his first subjects
for elevation
What an ideal place to plant seed for a new
vampire nation
There was no escape and they would breathe
his virus deep into their lungs
Their bloodstream would take it far beyond
It would not begin to take effect for several
days
Not all would be transformed and some not
even fazed

Vampire Sapien

D T Pollard

Those with a healthy immune system may
not fall
Mumbai knew disease was always present
and his virus would conquer all
Bodies trying to repel some foreign enemy
The strain would persist and Vampire
Sapien they would be
It was an opportunistic hunter and could
long survive
Those stricken with serious ailments would
revive
Cancers and other ailments would be
defeated
Mumbai's strain was pure and could not be
treated
It had strength like the lion and strikes like
the snake
The miracle of rebirth as a Vampire Sapien
was being truly awake
As they matured their view of how they
perceived their fellow man
Would change from equal to prey to exploit
when they can

Mumbai peered downward and saw a
sea of lights
This machine carrying him
descended in flight
Once he exited with his slaves
leading the way
Mumbai was taken to a hotel to stay
This place was strange and confused
his mind
Towering buildings, blaring sound
and blinding lights he did find
This Vampire Sapien had to conquer
his fears
Of being obsolete after three hundred
years
He fought back his anxiety and
buried his doubting notions
Mumbai would not fail after crossing
a vast ocean
"You two have perform your task
well
Delivering me to where many
humans dwell
This is where I will cast my virus far
and wide
New York will become a place
where Vampire Sapiens need not
hide
Those I seeded on what you call an
airplane will hear my call

Vampire Sapien   D T Pollard

In coming days I will meet with
them all
They will not understand what is
taking place
Their bodies will burn and changes
will occur in their faces
The roofs of their mouths will begin
to ache and their teeth will hang
It will be the formation of a canal
sheathing their fangs
They will run and for two days hide
Until the transformation is complete,
their fangs will remain inside
We do not appear any different than
a normal man
Our true nature appears only when it
can
My teeth appear to be just as any
Homo Sapien and are no longer
But they move aside when my
canines are required to slash and
rend to feed my hunger"

"Master Mumbai all of the people on
the flight did not remain here
Some flew elsewhere both far and
near
How will you teach them, how can
they be found
What will they do if you are not
around?"
Miles asked his master with a hint of
fright
He was still confused since
conversion on that African night
"It is of no concern
The virus is pure and on their own
they will learn
Inside the virus' core, all of the
knowledge does lie
Like a snake knows to bite without
being told to try
Vampire Sapiens are from the day
they are born
Destined to do what is a is a Vampire
Sapien norm
Vampire Sapiens do not emerge until
the age of ascension
It is only then that they enter a new
dimension
Two score and five is when that day
arrives
Until that time they live human lives

They will live, love and even breed
Unbeknownst to them, spreading the
seed
I will need some time to study this
age
I need to understand the new ways
before I write this fresh page
Of history for my ancient race
It will begin in this vast place."
For one month Mumbai did watch,
study and read
Until he understood the things he
would need
Then when that time had passed with
days one by one
Mumbai emerged uttering, "It is
done."

Vampire Sapien   D T Pollard

"I feel my offspring's' beckoning
calls
Tonight I shall go to meet them all
An abandoned structure shall be the
place
There, their creator, they will face."
After the sun had long ceased
illuminating the earth
Mumbai ran to meet the first brood
after their rebirth
At a time when most would be
asleep
Mumbai flexed his muscles with a
final fifty-foot leap
Then deep into a dark city night
One by one the newlings filed in,
what a glorious sight
When then number reached one
hundred and ten
Mumbai stood above them all, and
said, "Welcome, my friends."
"What has happened to us?" said one
from the crowd
Jonathan Mumbai stood, stretched
his frame and said out loud
"You are human no more
We are now members of a new
Vampire Sapien core"
Mumbai was about to speak and hit
his stride

When suddenly a new figure burst
inside
This monster stood over seven feet
tall
It began to smash and crash the new
vampires into the walls
Mumbai roared and cleared his head
He looked around and all of his new
brood was dead
This thing that stood before him did
not seem right
The Vampire Sapien braced for a
fight
"Who are you?" Mumbai asked the
monstrous freak
"I am the nightmare you dream of
when you sleep."
"I know who you are Jonathan
Mumbai
This may be the night that you die
I don't think that I will kill you now
I am Regan, you remember my
father, Donovan Krakow
When you fought him, he failed to
mention
His son, who had not yet reached the
age of ascension"
"I killed Krakow and cut off his head
I was the last one after he was dead."
"Mumbai, you are a relic and can not
survive

Vampire Sapien   D T Pollard

This is a new world that will eat you
alive
Krakow, had loved one other
After my birth you slaughtered my
mother."

"Your mother, can you tell me how
I killed your mother as you stand
there now"
Oh I think that you can recall
A woman that you killed who stood
six feet tall
She was blond and like no other
You killed her dead and consumed
my brother."
"I did not kill your mother that is a
lie
The blond woman, I killed, a few
months ago, she did die"
"Mumbai you were gone for
hundreds of years
My mother's ascension was delayed
by tears
Father's death drove her to sorrow
She decided to see countless
tomorrows
A normal human would have long
met death
Bearing my brother's fetus renewed
her health
She traveled to Africa to seek you
out
To ask you, what your battle with my
father was about
You butchered her body and tore her
apart

Vampire Sapien   D T Pollard

Then consumed my brother and
hardened my heart
Now Mumbai, here you stand
Claiming to save Vampire Sapiens,
all at your hand
No one summoned you or called for
a savior
We need no return of your barbaric
behavior
You are lost and I see
That the only Vampire Sapiens left
are you and me
I have worked for three hundred and
ten years
To dilute our strain and end our fears
This can be a wonderful place
But it does not need a separate
Vampire Sapien race
There are vampire trait carriers all
around
Yet the strain is weak and can not be
found
That is my dream and aspiration
Vampire Sapiens will achieve
complete human assimilation."

Mumbai's eyes did burn with fire
Such blasphemous words did raise
his ire
"What manner of Vampire are you
You prevent me from completing
what I was born to do
Now you stand to block my grandest
creation
The rebirth of a separate vampire
nation"
"Stop Mumbai, you speak of
madness
What you seek will lead to sadness
You have not witnessed the humans'
modern weapons
Your thoughts of a separate peace is
but a deception
We would be rounded up and hunted
down
There would not be a place where we
could not be found
If you insist, then we must
Decide this in combat in three weeks
at dusk
Our battle will range far and wide
From me you can not hide
The city will shake, the ground will
rock
In three weeks we meet in mortal
combat by the sea at the docks
If man detects us, then he will see

The greatest battle in Vampire
Sapien history."
"Krakow, I must inquire, why are
you so grotesque?
Vampire Sapiens are strong, lean and
without bulging flesh."
"I have prepared to meet you for
three hundred years
You are centuries older and I had to
conquer my fears
I indulged in chemicals designed by
man
To build my body and strengthen my
hand."
"Krakow I take my leave
Three weeks hence, you will bleed."
"Krakow, to be sure, you are a
disgrace
To me, your father and the entire
Vampire Sapien race."

Vampire Sapien   D T Pollard

"I must hone my skill
This scion of Krakow is destined to kill
I am far removed from the lion Mukanda
I must travel to the frozen tundra
Another combatant I must find, yes I know
I will go to where bears are as white as snow
Man's winged metal beast will take me there
I will spend two weeks sparring with a white
bear
I will return before three weeks have passed
To battle Regan Krakow, the die was cast."
Jonathan Mumbai traveled to a far off land
The edge of civilization was at hand
Northern Alaska was a harsh and
unforgiving place
Mumbai walked alone to seek an opponent
to face
At last he viewed a sea of white
A windswept terrain lay before his sight
Then he recoiled at the sight before his eyes
A solitary boar of monumental size
This beast was thrice Mukanda's weight
Yet he walked with a graceful gate
He stopped, lifted his head and sniffed the
air
This bear sensed a strange creature and
raised his hair
Mumbai stepped into full view
This bear stared and decided what to do
He approached Mumbai and was not
discreet

Vampire Sapien   D T Pollard

Three paces away, he stood on his hind legs
and towered over ten feet
"What do they call you?" said the vampire
"Toloch, Who are you to inquire?
What kind of creature can speak to me?
What manner of human can you be?"
"I am a Vampire Sapien, last of the pure
I am no threat to your kingdom, of that you
can be sure
I prepare to face an enemy in an epic fight
I ask to battle you to build my might
In gratitude I will bring you prey
I pledge two seals every day"
Toloch set his massive front paws onto the
snow
His answer was delivered with a massive
right paw blow
Mumbai was amazingly caught unaware
The vampire flew ten feet into the air
Mumbai had never felt such raw power
He fought the white bear for ten straight
hours

Vampire Sapien   D T Pollard

Mumbai was rocked by this awesome bear's
strength
He knew this would prepare for the conflict
ten days hence
The vampire kept to his part of the deal
Every day he delivered the bear a duo of
seals
Of the flesh he did also devour
It served as pure energy and built his power
One day before Mumbai was to depart
He told Toloch to fight with all of his heart
"Mumbai are you certain you can survive
The unleashed power of the greatest
carnivore alive?"
"White bear this is why I am here
I must be tested and have no fear
Let us have one final release
Then I must travel back to the east."
"Vampire, prepare yourself and steel your
back
I will battle you as if under another bear's
attack."
Toloch started with a furious rush
One and a half tons designed to crush
He pounded Mumbai with two paws into his
chest
The vampire withstood, and brought the
great bear's charge to rest
Toloch attempted a bite in Mumbai's neck
kill zone

Vampire Sapien   D T Pollard

Jonathan grasped jaws with his hands that
could crush bone
Then in a maneuver that proved his goal
complete
Mumbai lifted the mighty ice bear off his
feet
The vampire threw Toloch five yards to the
side
He rolled in the snow with his mouth open
wide
"Vampire you have impressed me with your
skill
There should be no man or beast that you
can not kill"
Mumbai bid his new friend goodbye
In two days a Vampire Sapien would die.

Jonathan Mumbai waited alone by the
abandoned dockside
Regan Krakow would have nowhere to hide
Then as if dropped from the sky
Krakow appeared and uttered a cry
He was adorned in armor from head to feet
Mumbai was unclothed that is the tradition
he would keep
"Krakow you are an animal with no vampire
pride
Behind man's armor, you try to hide
You will find that it will be to no avail
Now is the time for you to wail."
Mumbai jumped forth with an inhuman leap
He crashed into Regan, sending him flying
into a heap
Krakow sprung up with furious rush
His intention was to finish Mumbai with his
strength and crush
About eight feet tall Krakow did stand
With muscles as taught as steel bands
With one swing he struck a crippling blow
Yet the weight of armor made him slow
Mumbai was a swift as the wind
He moved aside and he did send
Regan forward and he did smash
Into a stack of steel cargo containers and
upon him they crashed
Mumbai decided it was time to increase the
fight

Krakow's son did not match his father's
might
When his enemy extricated himself from the
rubble
He realized he was in severe trouble
As soon as he reared his head and stood
Mumbai smashed his helmet with a massive
timber of wood
The metal helmet did move and twist
Mumbai pummeled Regan in the abdomen
with his fists
A Vampire Sapien of over two thousand
years
Has knuckles like steel and very few fears
Regan's armor began to bend and crack
Jonathan continued his vicious attack
The son of Krakow valiantly tried to survive
Deep down he sensed, this was his last night
alive
Mumbai took a powerful swing from below
The impact removed Regan's helmet with
one swift blow
Regan fell flat on his back
His throat was exposed for one last attack
Mumbai pounced and his fangs sank in
Ripping out Krakow's windpipe and this
fight was at an end
Now to ensure that his enemy was dead
Mumbai, Vampire Sapien born, remove
Regan's head
Then there was a startling sight

Vampire Sapien   D T Pollard

From above a noise and blinding light
"Don't move, or I'll shoot you where you
stand."
That was the voice of some unseen man
Jonathan Mumbai held the severed head and
dove into the sea
He swam into the darkness, no one knew
where he could be
Mumbai swam twenty miles and walked
onto dry sand
He gathered driftwood and built a fire with
his hands
Once the flames reached the temperature he
would need
He tossed Regan's head into the inferno and
completed the deed
Now that his deadly tasks were completed
for the day
Mumbai walked into the ocean and swam
away.

Vampire Sapien   D T Pollard

Act 4

Loneliness descended over Mumbai as he
swam to the east in despair
He had failed and needed time for his spirit
to repair
Raising a new nation of Vampire Sapiens
had escaped his reach
That city, New York, he left behind had hard
lessons to teach
Now that the body of young Krakow
Rested in human hands now
Man would discover that he was not alone
He would use his science to examine, dissect
and dismember Krakow down to his bones
Then he would know of the others that came
from Eden's garden
Not man, not beast but higher than each and
humans' hearts' will harden
Could he think it was one of his legendary
beasts of lore
Sasquatch, Yeti or the missing link that was
no more
Mumbai continued to swim across the
waters of the Atlantic
His strokes were powerful and sure, yet his
thoughts were frantic
A Vampire Sapien controls every cell of his
body and he swam in an undulating motion

Vampire Sapien   D T Pollard

He commanded the flesh on his hands and
feet to flatten as he powered across the
ocean
With hands as broad as paddles and feet
flattened like flippers, underwater would
Mumbai glide
Jonathan moved through the water more like
a dolphin riding at a ship's side
His skin extracted oxygen from the waters
of the deep and he increased his speed
There were no rules of human limitations
the he needed to heed
All night and all day the vampire did swim
After traversing over two thousand miles he
once again felt earth underneath him
Mumbai stood and walked from the sea
An island near Bermuda, just where he
thought he would be
This allowed him to rest and feed
A massive ship built for pleasure anchored
nearby provided just what he would need
Sustenance came to him as he rested on a
desolate beach
Two lovers seeking hidden moments came
within the vampire's reach
Mumbai struck them as the two lovers were
kissing
They simply became two more tourists
suddenly missing
In the mysterious history of Bermuda it was
an added another test

Vampire Sapien   D T Pollard

Mumbai for one full day did rest
Jonathan walked into the ocean until he
could be seen no more
Swimming towards South Africa and a
distant shore
Somewhere along his journey as he glided in
a state near sleep
A great body emerged from the deep
It moved under the vampire and with a
fatigued gasp
He grasped onto the thick skin and with his
chiseled fingernails Mumbai did clasp
Mumbai attached himself in the dark of
night
Like a great parasitic fish and rested to
regain his might
The vampire ride rode the back of the great
blue whale
When the behemoth surfaced Mumbai
would grasp a fish and feed without fail
For days he was a passenger and regained
his strength
As the enormous leviathan reached the
equator it was time to swim the final length
The whale continued south and Mumbai
departed from the beast
His target was in mind and he swam to the
east
Mumbai was returning to Africa from
whence he came

Vampire Sapien   D T Pollard

He needed to reflect as this world was not
the same
He needed to plan his next actions and
decide if the die was cast
Was the age of Vampire Sapiens in the
distant past
Was it time to end the strain
Jonathan spent days swimming through the
Atlantic until his muscles were in pain
Finally he entered the Indian Ocean and felt
a hint of pride
That he was near his destination as South
Africa was on his left side
The Cape of Good Hope marked a soon
northward turn
East became north and Mumbai continued
his furious churn
Now framed by two masses of land
Africa and Madagascar's beaches of sand
Then at last Mumbai saw his destination
Kenya, at last, his home, now a nation
As he neared, the shore loomed before his
eyes
Suddenly he was airborne and viewing the
skies
The vampire landed on a sandy shore
He turned and peered out to the ocean and

out of the depths arose a sight never seen
before

With a mouth of a lion and the head of a
bear
Its body resembled a leopard with short
brown hair
Seven tentacles extended from its body long
and thin
Each one contained something resembling a
human head at the end
Ten hornlike protrusions extended from the
shoulder of this beast
This creature was twenty feet tall at the least
Located under the lion-shaped mouth was
the head of a man
"Mumbai, why do you look so surprised
don't you recognize me, come closer if you
can
You recall tossing my head into the sea and
thought I was dead
A great white shark consumed my head
I am Donovan Krakow."
"How could it be you standing there now?
Three hundred years have passed since I left
your body to rot
How could you be alive, this is some dream,
is it not
What kind of monster have you come to
be?"
"I became one with the shark and he one
with me
I controlled his life, his thoughts and
movement

Vampire Sapien   D T Pollard

My genes fused with his the longer time
went
I made my plans and waited my turn
For three centuries I planed everything so I
could watch you burn
You condemned me to live in the seas
I had no limbs to walk and no lungs to
breathe
Yet, year by year I grew to suit my need
I swallowed a bull shark and from the sea I
was freed
I could then swim waters free of salt
That allowed my plan to grow without halt."
"Krakow I will hear no more."
"No, Vampire, you will hear it all, before I
place you at death's door
I added to my genetic pool
I found a polar bear swimming twenty miles
away from land and it was a perfect tool
I consumed him and that freed me from the
waters and seas
I never knew how glorious that first step on
land would be
Lungs and limbs allowed me to walk and
inhale air
One by one they fell from shark to bear
Lion, leopard and octopus were added to us,
each was targeted and consumed without fail
My horns came from the Narwhal whale."
Mumbai asked "What manner of madness is
in your heart?"

Vampire Sapien   D T Pollard

"Mumbai you have been away for three
hundred years, you don't know where to
start
Man has unlocked his greatest fears
He discovered the power of our smallest
essence and unleashed many tears
It was used twice against his own
While you slumbered, man built nuclear
bombs and away, his own kind was blown
He attached those nightmare weapons to
great rockets that can pierce the skies
Now they are aimed at each other and if
used, everyone dies
The only thing stronger than man's
destructive might
Is their belief in religion, the source of
endless fights
Our relative's wars never cease
Some based upon greed, and others based
upon sovereign beliefs
One road leads to heaven, the other leads to
hell
It all depends on what their God decreed if
the world fell
I will emerge from the Mediterranean Sea
On the western shores of Israel is where they
will see me
Men will tremble and lust for the kill
Churches, Synagogues and Mosques will fill

Vampire Sapien   D T Pollard

I will be called The Beast and man's
Revelation will be fulfilled on the battlefield
of Armageddon."
Doomsayers will reach for their holy books
and say, "Destiny has won."
"You have been driven to madness Krakow,
you are a living lie."
"Silence! Mumbai.
Men will marshal their armies, choose
allegiance and select a side
Their destined conflagration will ensue and
when it is over millions will have died
Their terrible weapons will be release from
the ground, air and sea
This world will burn and those left will
tremble and gather around me
The survivors will cast their loyalties with
me and they will sing
I will be their savior, master and king."
"Enough with your mad ramblings,
Krakow!"
Mumbai rushed the abomination and took a
incredible leap yelling, "I will kill you again,
now."
He severed one of Krakow's head like
appendages and blood did stream
Krakow unleashed a loud and deafening
scream
Jonathan Mumbai began to run to the north
and west

Vampire Sapien   D T Pollard

He knew his speed would put Krakow to the
test
He was much faster than the monster
accustomed to water bearing his weight
Mumbai ran for twelve hours and placed
miles between himself, Krakow and their
ultimate fate
Mumbai stopped in the midst of a vast
grassland, crouched and surveyed
He sensed eyes hidden in the tall blades
The he saw blended into the brown
vegetation
Hairs from a regal mane of a male lion,
king of this animal nation
"Vampire, I see that your senses are still
sharp."
"Mukanda, you yet live, it gladdens my
heart."
"Yes, I live. I dominate this grassy plain
My question is where is the rest of your
Vampire Sapien strain?"
"Old friend I will explain later on another
day
Right now a nightmare comes this way
Within half a sun cycle, he will be here
If he is not stopped, all life on earth will live
in fear
No beast or man will escape what he will
bring to pass
I will combat him alone if I must, but I need
your animal kingdom's forces to amass

Vampire Sapien   D T Pollard

I know every lion here has their own
territory and pride
And you deign not to trespass, yet that will
not matter if you all died
Mukanda, I implore you to call to your
rivals and we are running out of time
To unite as one and form a secondary line
In the event I fail to prevail
You need to lead your legion in mass to
destroy the nightmare following my trail."
"Mumbai, I sense that your concern is great
You are not one prone to exaggerate
I will call to my brethren to come in droves
Both pride kings and bachelor rouges."

Vampire Sapien   D T Pollard

Mumbai used the time to prepare his mind
In this twist of fate he could save mankind
He found a quiet space under the shade of a
tree
There he kneeled on one knee
Then from the river he did drink deep
Crocodiles lurked, waiting on a hapless
victim to creep
Then at an hour with the sun sinking low
Mukanda with his army did show
Standing in the distance were five prides
Forty-five loins standing side by side
Behind the lions were four adult bull
elephants towering above the rest
Mumbai reviewed this corps that nature sent
and hoped they could meet the test
Then as if on some hidden cue
Krakow standing treetop tall, broke through
The surrounding forest into the clear
His appearance startled the lions, but created
no fear
Mumbai looked up to the sky and the ground
below
He pondered if there was a heaven where
vampires go
"Mumbai now is the time for you to die
I see you have assembled an audience to
watch you suffer and cry."
"Krakow, talk is at an end
This final battle shall begin."

Vampire Sapien   D T Pollard

Krakow moved forward and swung his
leopard's paw
Mumbai moved to one side, yet was struck
in the side by his sharpened claws
His skin was ripped and flesh did show
With a pain tolerance no human could know
Jonathan never ceased his motion and
jumped very high
He rushed Krakow and smashed into his
head from the sky
This was as focused as a Vampire Sapien
could be
Fighting an opponent much stronger than he
There was not any restraint or reservation
Mumbai felt Krakow was no longer of the
Vampire Sapien nation
This could be his legacy but no one would
understand
If he prevailed, a vampire would save the
world of man
Then like a nightmare that lives in the night
Krakow did grasp Mumbai and took flight
There was no doubt it seemed
This creature possessed the ability to sprout
wings
Mumbai knew he could not allow Krakow to
gain high altitude
He did something very brutal and crude
Donovan Krakow sought to squeeze away
Mumbai's breath
That was one true way to bring on death

Mumbai recalled his battles with the ice bear
He knew how he built his strength there
"Krakow I managed to kill your son
Once you are dead, your line will be done."
"You lie and are a blasphemous dog."
Mumbai was in a haze and looking through
a fog
Yet as Krakow continued to speak
Jonathan grasped Krakow's jaws before he
became too weak."
With one mighty effort Mumbai pulled his
jaws apart
He exerted with all of the strength of his
vampire heart
As Mumbai lost consciousness from a lack
of air
Krakow's jaws came apart with a horrific
tear
The death grip was released from Mumbai's
frame
He knew the end time had came
Jonathan clasped his enemy as they fell to
the ground
Mumbai severed Krakow's head and peace
he found
As he witnessed the rapid approach of the
surface below
There was no way to prepare for the
tremendous blow
The impact was as none he ever knew

Vampire Sapien   D T Pollard

This was the end and there was nothing else
to do
Even with bones as hard as steel
A plunge from ten thousand feet was
destined to kill
Mumbai and Krakow smashed into the earth
with a sickening sound
Donovan Krakow broke into three large
pieces littered all around
Jonathan Mumbai crashed and tumbled into
solid stones
His body was a twisted mass of broken
bones
Mukanda ran to the vampire to inquire
"Mukanda, you must destroy my body in
fire
I saw smoke in the distance where the
grasslands burn now
Deposit my body and the head of the
monster Krakow
In the path of the advancing flames with
brush piled high
The new age of Vampire Sapiens will the
flames deny
Toss Krakow's body into the river that flows
The crocodiles will be quick to dispose."
"Yes my friend, I will do as you ask
My comrades, the elephants are up to the
task."
Mukanda beckoned to two massive elephant
males

Vampire Sapien

D T Pollard

They approached Mumbai and their tusks
did not fail
Huge curved tusks scooped up the remains
of Krakow
They were tossed into the river and it was up
to the crocodiles now
Twenty-foot water monsters tugged at the
carcass with all of their might
Furious death rolls ripped Krakow into
pieces amid a furious fight
Mumbai clutched Krakow's head to his
chest and looked up
One of the elephants scooped him up with
his curved tusks
Mukanda led the bull towards an orange
glow to the east
Two hours later, the vampire was placed on
the ground by the lumbering beast
Jonathan Mumbai lay in the grass with
Krakow's head at his side
The flames roared toward him like an
incoming tide
Mukanda and the bull covered the vampire
with brush
Time was short and they had to rush
Mumbai looked into the starry night sky
He knew it was time for the Vampire Sapien
race to die
With all of his strength he took one last
breath in

Vampire Sapien   D T Pollard

Mumbai exhaled the last of his Vampire
Sapien viral spores into the wind
Mukanda looked the vampire in his eyes and
spoke true
"Vampire you know what I must do."
Then in one swift and furious bite
Mumbai's throat was removed swiftly
without a fight
The lion and elephant ran to escape
Flames approaching at a furious rate
Then Jonathan Mumbai, Vampire Sapien
with pure desire
Was consumed in nature's funeral pyre
In an inferno caused by a lightning strike
Vampire Sapiens, a cousin of man, existence
ended that African night.

About The Author

ESSENCE® bestselling author D.T. Pollard lives in the Dallas/Fort Worth, TX area. He is married and has one son.

He earned an academic scholarship to the School of Business and Industry at Florida A & M University. He stopped writing during his second year in college.

D T was at the top of his class in Marketing and graduated Summa Cum Laude and won the Most-Outstanding-Performance-in-Marketing award for his graduating class of 1981.

While working in sales for giants of the high-technology world for over 28 years, his desire to write returned after losing several siblings from various causes. D T Pollard is the author of Rooftop Diva - A Novel of Triumph After Katrina, Fools' Heaven – Love, Lust and Death beyond the Pulpit, TARP Town U S A – The Recession That Saved America and OBAMA – GUILTY – of Being President While Black, The Mark Unmasked and Publish Free For Kindle Today – Sell Worldwide Tomorrow.